SPRING CLEANING

A COLLECTION OF REFLECTIONS

Misty Verna

BookLeaf
Publishing

India | USA | UK

Spring Cleaning

A Collection of Reflections

© 2021 Misty Verna

Presentation by *BookLeaf Publishing*

Web: www.bookleafpub.com

E-mail: info@bookleafpub.com

ISBN: 9789358360592

First edition 2021

To my fellow creatives who encourage me to open up and express myself: thank you, you mean the world to me.

Preface

Springtime is for renewal of life, whether that be physical, mental or emotional. This is just a small selection from my own personal journey of finding new life in the new season. I hope that you find some of these words resonate with you and comfort you when needed.

Always remember, you are not alone.

1

there is a distinct chill in the air today

it caresses my shoulders like a past
lover

yet i shiver just the same

gusts feel cold and calculated

as they laugh and turn away

i wonder how i got here

yet i shiver just the same

spring cleaning

cleansing the cold out of the air

removing the feeling of stale memories

moving on from them

i am trying to clear the cobwebs from my
space

only to realize that the spiders won't
stop

spinning and spinning and

weaving webs in my brain that even
spring cleaning can't control

i wish i was whole

instead of wholly incomplete

i wish i could run

but instead i am sleepwalking

i wish i could hear

but instead my ears ring out like sirens

i wish i could live

but instead i bury my dreams

dreaming of the day when home is

no longer a bad word

rather, it will entice me with its walls

ones that harbor music instead of
calamity

ones that i can make my own with
expression

ones that are insulated with love and
acceptance

if the stars align for you

will they align for me, too?

or will they simply shine down

on my transgressions?

a divine dissection of my

tainted and tattered soul

i'm sorry if i'm rambling and obsessing
over my

mistakes and my words and my feelings
and my life that feels like it's spiraling
out of control but

all i want is for the stars to align for me

so i can feel the universe working

ripping the weeds out of my mind is like

sawing through all of the connections
and pretending i know how to sort them
out

drowning the weeds in my mind won't do
any good when

i'd just as easily drown myself too

my hourglass is widening its core

the sand hurries its flow and i begin to cough

how did i get here?

it feels like i've simply survived

treading heavy water under my aching feet

i'm on an endless beach and the tide is rising

a storm of responsibility and i can't swim

how do i get out of here?

i just want to watch the sunset

before it fades into darkness

where is the fine line that lives

between romance and friendship?

loneliness lurks underneath my skin's
surface

a dull itch where i long for attention and
affection

will it ever subside? will it ever be cared
for?

or will the skin simply crack and bleed
out every ounce of hope it had for a
commitment?

platonic love is just as vital to fill a void

but it's simply not the same

femininity is a double-edged sword

one that curses and soothes those

who embrace it

it strengthens those around us and

simultaneously breaks us down until

the ultimate realization is made

women owe nothing to those who act
like they deserve everything

and women only owe themselves

the peace of mind that comes with
self-love

chipping away at myself like the
black polish staining my fingernails

i slowly chip away at my ego

my self-image

my battlefield of a mind

slowly but surely setting aside hope that

one day i'll find something beautiful
under the chipped away
pieces of myself

drowsy dreams of disaster

make my skin crawl and my heart pound

what does the unconscious know
that i don't?

i want to dive into that trove of
unknown terror

and discover for myself what my brain is
hiding from me

sleepy eyes mask a world of digested
demons

they only appear when the world is
drifting away

candy is sweet until the bitter end

it entices more and more until you're

trapped in the sickly sweet cycle

teeth can only withstand so much

before they chip and crack
under the pressure of

candy that's sweet until the bitter end

we are not alone in the
experience of loneliness

irrationality doesn't change the fact that
the feeling of isolation is feeling like

drowning in water that you don't know
how to swim in so you just stay there

lungs burning, stomach churning

willing to do anything to stop the
sinking feeling

but drowning nonetheless

i have been trying to try but

loneliness creeps in and

dissolves my efforts with

its abrasive sting

and i am sinking

drowning in

the deep

down

dark

if only i learned my lesson the first time
but here i am with wings
torn and tattered

crawling back to the same old space

causing the same trouble
in the same place

people play the part of persistence

trying to help me, trying to listen

but god only knows how useless
ubiquitous petitions are when god only
helps those who help themselves

how is it that the universe feels
so vast and so small all at once?

perspective shifts like water in a glass

wavy and misleading

it always leaves me wondering
if there's more

the clock ticks away endlessly as i
struggle to steep tea

the witches' brew in my brain bubbles away
until it flows from my eyes and my words
words that form a mask to shield my faces
from the hardness of my pillow and the
flames that lash out from
too-well-known places

a masquerade it is, a dance
on eggshells that crumble underneath the
heavyweight in my head
that beats my heart to shreds
playing the fool that hasn't read
the warning signs that lie among the plants
in the jungle i am lost in

navigating through the tossing and the
turning
trying to decipher between yearning and
searching
for something more than myself
more than my health
more than this endless cycle

the clock ticks away endlessly as i
just want to go to sleep.

i wish my mind would make itself up

i could gather my thoughts from the dark
corners in which they settled and arrange
them to form some sort of coherency

fill in the gaps between my consciousness
my beliefs are strung together with cheap
thread and it's well-worn

i wish i could make my own decisions
instead of relying on my mind's anxieties
and the hypocritical smiles of others

how do i look for truth behind their selfish
masks?

i refuse to be dragged behind another
untrustworthy leader, a captor
running rampant through the broken streets
and saving few faces while destroying
countless ones
who do i believe in a whirlwind of
deception?

i wish my mind felt free
i wish my mind was free

i want the wind to carry me away
to put me in a different place
and show me how i can
live in a different way

i want my hair to blow freely
i want to feel it whipping around
my face as i
stand in the pouring rain and
soak it into my skin
i want to be drenched with motivation
and inspiration to be the
best version of myself

i want the air to fill my lungs
i want to feel the rise and
fall of my chest
without an accompanying sense of
anxiety
i want to breathe the outside air
the same air that moves
in and out of us all
the atmosphere above that grounds us
with the hopeful earth below

the heart is a resilient vessel
it holds the emotions the brain resists
pumping them full of life and energy

when the vessel is shattered
broken bloody bits are scattered
and tourniquets are tattered

but the heart is a resilient vessel
repairable like gilded ceramics
shining through the night like stars

prisms bend light

and make beautiful rainbows out of it

i have been bent by the wind

and i hope i can

make something beautiful out of it

i used to live with smoke and mirrors
for shelter

i found refuge in their lies

they built them up around me until i
could only see my clouded eyes

the smell of smoke still lingers
and broken mirrors are on the floor

though i no longer live with
smoke and mirrors
i continue to cough more and more

what is it worth to you?
what am i worth to you?

 is worth even anything more than a
deconstructive construct?

one that skews our views of ourselves
and our world and
our universe and beyond

what is anything
or anyone
if not for its worth?

that being said
what is it worth to you?
what am i worth to you?

fortune follows those who
walk in new adventures daily

sharp teeth only sink into those who
stomp on the feet of those around them

tread lightly and be wary of thorns

the kind that dig deep into the soul

and bury themselves in the blood

silence is silvery in the moonlight
it is calm yet deafening when
all you hear is the roaring of your head

silence is peaceful in the sunshine
it is interrupted by the buzzing of bees
and the singing of birds
in the rustling trees

silence shifts with our perspective
sometimes peaceful
sometimes paranoid

but silence is stillness nevertheless

maybe i'll meet someone
with golden eyes and a heart to match

matches ignite flames behind my chest
and in my throat

it's suffocating

maybe i'll meet someone
with a silver tongue that wraps
around my neck until it chokes me

it's suffocating

maybe i'll meet someone
with an iridescent smile
one that shifts when the lighting
changes and haunts me when
no one else is looking

it's suffocating

maybe i'll meet someone
or maybe i won't

never did i think i would feel this way

nostalgic

no memories of good times can
bring them back

but i can hope for the best

and i can dream of smiling days ahead

feeling alive is feeling vulnerable yet happy

it's driving with windows down
wind and leaves rushing in and rustling hair

it's staring at the stars and wondering
if being alone is a senseless myth

it's dancing in the rain without care
letting the water dissolve anxieties

feeling alive is feeling desperately hopeful

i caught myself being wistful again

wondering if the wind were to
whisk me away
where would i go?
what would i find over the rainbow?

would there be bluebirds and lemon drops
or buzzards and acid rain?

would i find myself in a fantasy
or dream in dystopia?

would my feet once again find solid ground?
would anyone wait for me to wake up?

some days it feels as though
anyone could just
walk through me

as if the tissue and bone were simply vapor
under pale skin, stretched thin
enough to see the hollowness inside

i wonder how many i pass
that i could simply pass through

vaporous shadows of my mind
drifting down like ghosts in the rain

i am an alien in my own life

slowly wandering away from the ship

leaving the others behind to sort the
wreckage of my makeshift metaphors

what does it mean to feel extraterrestrial?

maybe someday i'll find my universe &
they'll find it in my scars like nebulas